DINOSAUR
mysteries

Written by Mary O'Neill
Illustrated & Designed by John Bindon

Library of Congress Cataloging-in-Publication Data

O'Neill, Mary.
   Dinosaur mysteries.

   Summary: Discusses how scientists have been able to
reconstruct the physical characteristics, habits, and
natural environment of various dinosaurs by studying
bones and other fossilized evidence.
    1. Dinosaurs—Juvenile literature . [1. Dinosaurs]
I. Bindon, John, ill.   II. Title.
QE862.D5054 1989   567.9'1   89-4789
ISBN 0-8167-1635-8 (lib. bdg.)
ISBN 0-8167-1636-6 (pbk.)

10   9 8 7 6 5 4 3 2 1

Troll Associates

About This Book...

We have known about dinosaurs since the early nineteenth century. This may seem like a long time to us, but it really isn't. The study of dinosaur life is very new compared to many other areas of science.

In recent times, we have learned many new things about these amazing creatures. But more questions remain. Were some dinosaurs warm-blooded? Did some give birth to live babies? How far did some dinosaurs roam over the face of the earth? What color was their skin? Which dinosaurs lived alone? Which traveled in giant herds? When did the dinosaurs disappear? Did they really all disappear—or are some still with us today?

These are just some of the mysteries scientists are trying to solve. They know more now than they ever did before. And in this book, you will read about what they know and what they might never know! So read on and enter a world of dinosaur mysteries...

Table of Contents

Rebuilding the Dinosaurs

How do scientists decide what dinosaurs looked and acted like? After all, these creatures lived during the *Mesozoic* (Mez-uh-ZO-ik) Era, between 225 and 65 million years ago! We don't have any living dinosaurs to study. Scientists who study the remains of these ancient animals are called *paleontologists* (PAY-lee-on-TULL-uh-jists). A better name for them might be detectives! Putting together a picture of the dinosaur world is like putting together a giant jigsaw puzzle—with most of the pieces missing.

Fossils—The Building Blocks

The scientist's picture of a dinosaur starts with the bones left behind when the creature died. Over millions of years, these bones become covered in rock. The bones themselves turn into rock as the real bone disappears. But the rock *fossil* left behind tells us exactly what the bone was like.

Whole dinosaur skeletons are rarely found. Usually, the bones are broken up and spread over a wide area. Sometimes, the bones of different animals are mixed together. Many pieces may be missing. Scientists must carefully remove these bone fossils from the rock they are trapped in. The pieces are studied and put together to make whole dinosaur skeletons. This process can take many years.

Dinosaur Footprints

Look at the different dinosaur footprints shown here. Which do you think were made by heavy creatures? Which were made by light dinosaurs? Can you tell if the animals walked on two legs or four?

A skeleton can tell us a lot about the animal it belongs to. We can guess how tall and long the creature was. We can tell if it walked on two legs or four. Scientists can also make good guesses about how much an animal weighed.

Apart from showing what dinosaurs looked like, the bones can tell us a little about how they lived. Some dinosaurs had sharp teeth and claws. This tells us they ate meat. Others had rows and rows of blunt teeth. These were good for chewing leaves and branches. The bones can also tell us about how some dinosaurs protected themselves. Dinosaurs that had plates, horns, or spikes would have been more difficult to attack.

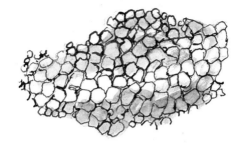

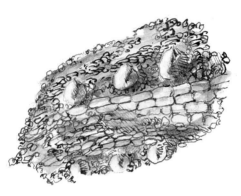

Working From the Inside Out

Paleontologists have to know a lot about today's living animals. Knowing how modern animals are built helps these scientists put the dinosaur bones together. Sometimes, they are lucky enough to work with bones that are in very good condition. These bones might have marks that show just where the muscles were attached. Scientists can then build the dinosaur models layer by layer.

One thing we don't know much about is dinosaur skin. The soft parts of animals usually do not survive as fossils. So we often must guess what the outsides of dinosaurs were really like.

Even Scientists Can Make Mistakes!

People don't always get things right when putting dinosaurs back together again. When the remains of plant-eating Iguanodon (Ig-WAN-oh-don) were first put together, the animal was shown with a horn on its nose. This "horn" was later found to be one of its thumbs.

Picturing the Dinosaurs' World

How do we know about the weather dinosaurs lived in? Was it hot or cold, wet or dry? How do we know what kinds of plants there were to eat? What other animals lived during the time of the dinosaurs?

There is much that scientists don't know about the dinosaur world, but the earth gives some clues. For instance, the earth's crust can tell them about how old the dinosaurs are. The surface of the earth is made up of layers. Each of these layers dates from a different time in the earth's history. The layer of rock a fossil is found in usually tells scientists how old the fossil is. They know that dinosaurs lived between 225 and 65 million years ago. This is because the oldest dinosaur bones were found in a layer of rock from 225 million years ago. The "youngest" dinosaur bones come from a layer 65 million years old.

The earth was a different place all those years ago. Some of today's *continents* were actually joined together during the Age of Dinosaurs. As the earth's surface moved, the continents broke apart. That's why some countries are not in the same place now as they were long ago.

The *climates* were different then too. A region that is forest now might have been hot desert when dinosaurs lived in it. Countries that are very cold today may have been quite warm and mild long ago.

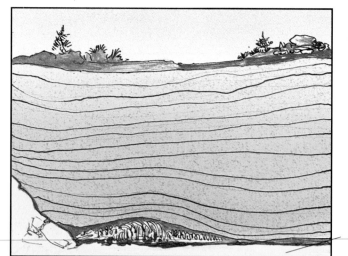

OVER MANY YEARS, ROCK AND SAND BUILD UP IN LAYERS COVERING THE DINOSAUR.

RIVERBED

6

Plant Clues

One clue to how warm a place was is the kinds of plants that grew there. Plants from millions of years ago left traces behind them. Some left imprints on stone just as this fern did. Certain kinds of seeds and pollen can also be found at fossil sites. Scientists can tell what kinds of plants they came from. They can tell from the plant life what the weather was like. The amount of plant fossils in an area also tells us about the weather. Many more plants grow in warm, wet areas than in cold or dry areas.

Scientists have another way of telling if the temperatures changed during the year. Fossils of wood show how much a tree grew each year by the rings in the tree's trunk. These tell scientists how long the growing season was each year. In a longer growing season, the tree rings were thicker. Trees do most of their growing when it is warm. So from these rings, scientists can guess how much of the year was warm and how much was cold.

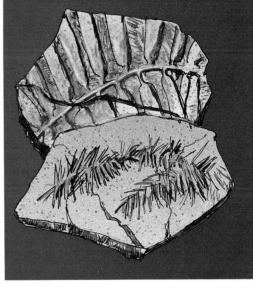

Be a Dinosaur Detective!

Two kinds of plant fossils are shown here. In what kinds of places do we find plants like these today? Which one do you think was from a warm climate and which from a cool climate?

Dinosaurs' Neighbors

Other creatures from the days of the dinosaurs have left traces behind. Fossils have been found that show the dinosaurs shared the earth with insects, fish, birds, other *reptiles*, small *mammals*, and *amphibians* (creatures that live part of their lives on land and part in water). These other kinds of animal fossils can tell scientists more about what dinosaurs ate, whom they competed with, and what the climate was probably like.

7

Dinosaur Fashions

Scientists have argued for a long time about what Stegosaurus (STEG-uh-SORE-us) really looked like. This big, slow-moving plant-eater lived about 150 million years ago. It had large triangular plates down its back that probably helped discourage enemies. Stegosaurus's tail also had wicked spikes that helped in fighting off meat-eaters.

Before, scientists disagreed about whether the back plates ran in two matching rows or two uneven rows. But now a dinosaur artist and paleontologist says there was only one row of plates down the animal's back.

Scientists used to think there were two rows of plates because of the way the plates seem to fit. The plates on the neck and shoulders have thick, overlapping bases. These made people think that in order to be balanced, there must be two rows down the back. People believed this, even though the most complete skeleton ever found had only one row of plates. Like most dinosaur fossils, this Stegosaurus had some parts missing. These were from its tail. So scientists just thought that some of its back plates were missing too.

The new model of Stegosaurus shows it with just one row of plates from its neck to its tail. The overlapping bases of the neck and shoulders hold plates that point up and outward. Stephen Czerkas is the man who has "rebuilt" Stegosaurus. He says that the overlapping bases let the dinosaur move more comfortably.

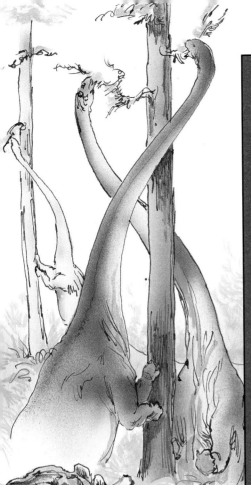

Stegosaurus—The Sunbather

The temperature had been cool during the night. Stegosaurus was feeling chilled to the bone. Her movements were stiff as she came awake and walked out of the bush to look around.

The sun was just coming up over the mountains. A few other sleepy-headed creatures were beginning to move about as well. It was a time when all moved carefully, keeping a lookout for dangerous meat-eaters. Stegosaurus was more reckless than most. She had her armor plates and spikes to protect her. Her life depended on them. She often wandered into the path of hungry meat-eaters. Still, only the fiercest hunter would attack a stegosaur.

A Brachiosaurus (BRAY-key-oh-SORE-us) herd that had appeared the day before were already busy eating from the tallest trees. By the day's end, the roof of the forest would be stripped bare. But Stegosaurus was more interested in the lower greens that were within her reach. She found herself a patch of ferns far enough from the long-necked plant-eaters to be left alone. She positioned herself so that the broad side of her back was toward the sun. Her tall plates could catch the sun's rays better this way. In no time, the warmth spread through her body.

Happily, she ate with not a care in the world. If the sun became too hot later, she would find a shady patch to doze in.

Were Dinosaurs Warm-Blooded Or Cold-Blooded?

Like all human beings, you have warm blood flowing in your veins. Having warm blood helps us to do many things that cold-blooded animals cannot do. Since dinosaurs were first discovered, they have been considered cold-blooded animals. But now, some scientists say they must have been warm-blooded. What difference would this make? Why do scientists think it is important to know so much about dinosaur blood?

Endotherms and Ectotherms

Warm-blooded animals can produce their own body heat. They do this with the energy they get from eating food. Animals who can control their own body temperatures are called *endotherms*. Birds are endotherms. So are mammals such as humans, horses, and whales.

Cold-blooded animals have to depend on heat from their surroundings to keep their bodies warm. If the weather is cool, these animals become inactive. If the weather stays cool, they may die. Cold-blooded animals also have to protect themselves from too much heat. On very hot days, they have to take to the shade. Animals that depend on the sun for their body heat are called *ectotherms*. These include fish, lizards and other reptiles, and amphibians like frogs and newts.

Changing the Way We Think About Dinosaurs

If dinosaurs were warm-blooded, we would have to change much of our thinking about them. Warm-blooded animals can survive in places that are too cold for ectotherms. Endotherms can keep up a much faster pace of life. They can travel farther than cold-blooded animals, too. Endotherms also have to eat more than ectotherms. So warm-blooded dinosaurs would have needed more food. If some dinosaurs were warm-blooded, they may have been a lot smarter than we first thought they were. All of this means we may have to throw out some of our ideas about why dinosaurs disappeared.

The Speedy Dinosaur

The discovery of a speedy little dinosaur convinced some scientists that certain dinosaurs were warm-blooded. The bones of this dinosaur were found in the late 1960s. It was given the name Deinonychus (Dine-ON-ik-us). This means "terrible claw." The animal got its name from a hooked claw on each of its hind·legs.The claw seemed to be made for slashing and tearing at other animals.

Scientists put together Deinonychus's small size and sharp claws. They decided this must have been a very fast hunter. They thought only a warm-blooded animal would have had the energy to move that quickly.

11

Growing Up Fast

Another pair of scientists studied the bones of dinosaurs. They compared them to the bones of warm-blooded birds and cold-blooded crocodiles. The dinosaur bones seemed more like the bird bones. Bird and mammal bones are full of small holes that are connected to their blood delivery system. The dinosaur bones also showed these holes.

Other scientists pointed out that turtle bones are riddled with holes. Turtles are cold-blooded. These other scientists also say that some small mammals have bones like crocodiles and other reptiles. So not all warm-blooded animals have bones that are full of holes.

Scientists looking at the dinosaur bones wondered if they might be like bird bones in another way. Bird and mammal bones grow very fast. So the scientists studied how fast the bones of Hadrosaurus (HAD-ruh-SORE-us) grew. They did this by comparing the bones of young and old Hadrosauruses. The scientists found that this plant-eating dinosaur grew nine feet in its first year! Today, only warm-blooded animals can grow this fast.

Does this prove for sure that dinosaurs were warm-blooded? Not at all. Those who think dinosaurs were cold-blooded say that they would have starved if they had been warm-blooded. Endotherms must eat up to ten times as much as ectotherms of the same size. Imagine giant Apatosaurus (Ah-PAT-uh-SORE-us) eating so much food with its tiny mouth. Perhaps only some dinosaurs, such as the small meat-eaters, were warm-blooded. Scientists will probably argue about this for many years.

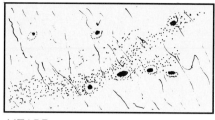

LIZARD

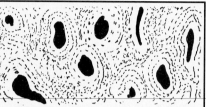

DINOSAUR

MAMMAL

Be a Dinosaur Detective!

Read over the story about Stegosaurus on page 9. What would make you think Stegosaurus was cold-blooded? How would the story be different if she were warm-blooded? Read the story about the Deinonychus pack on page 13. Do you think they were warm-blooded or cold-blooded? Why?

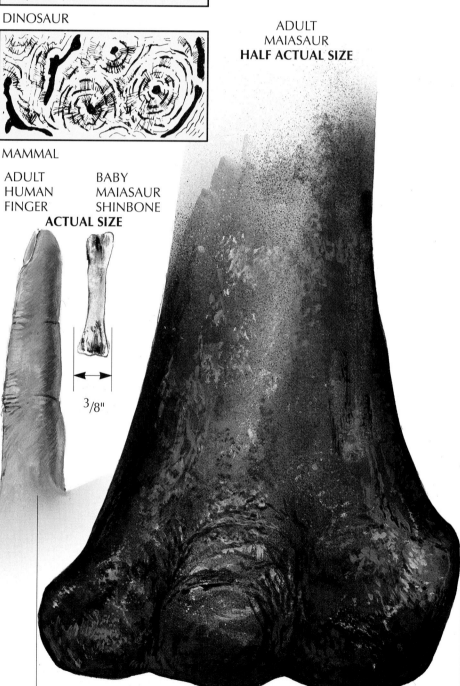

ADULT MAIASAUR
HALF ACTUAL SIZE

ADULT HUMAN FINGER

BABY MAIASAUR SHINBONE

ACTUAL SIZE

3/8"

9"

Deinonychus—The Surprise Attack

It was late evening when the Deinonychus pack picked up the teasing scent on the wind. Somewhere nearby was prey. The smell was strong. There was a great deal of food to be had. In the last week, the Deinonychus pack had only come across small forest animals. They were hungry now for a large kill.

They moved carefully upwind, following the scent. It took them to a clearing in the forest a little higher up. The hunters grew more and more excited as they drew near. The scent was from a group of Iguanodon—easy prey for

Deinonychus. Best of all, the quiet plant-eaters were nesting.

At the sight of the meat-eaters, the Iguanodon panicked. Their best escape from attackers was to flee. But some hesitated,not wanting to leave their eggs behind. The Deinonychus pack leapt upon these trailing animals. The meat-eaters worked well as a hunting team. With their light frames and strong limbs, they jumped easily onto the backs of the Iguanodon. Their sharp claws tore and ripped at their prey's flesh. Deinonychus had a special weapon—a giant hooked claw on each hind leg. It

went deep into their victims.

The plant-eaters fought back. Their greater size and sharp thumbs were some help. A few members managed to shake off their attackers. Before escaping, they gouged at the eyes of the Deinonychus pack and stabbed their limbs.

In minutes, the attack was over. Only one of the hunters had died. Many more had suffered stabs and slashings. The Deinonychus pack had done well. Five Iguanodon and a field of eggs lay waiting to be eaten.

Dinosaurs Out In the Cold?

Picture in your mind the world the dinosaurs lived in. You're probably imagining steamy swamps and huge ferns. Now try to imagine the dinosaurs in a snowstorm! It's hard to do, but some scientists think that certain dinosaurs might have lived in cold weather. Until recently, it was thought that these ancient giants could not live in cool parts of the world. But there have been new discoveries in far-off regions that show dinosaurs might have lived in the cold and dark.

Popping Up in Strange Places

Recent fossil finds in Antarctica, Argentina, Alaska, and southern Australia have scientists scratching their heads. Even during the Age of Dinosaurs, at least parts of these regions were within the Arctic or Antarctic Circle. This means they were probably cold. It is also likely they did not get much sunshine during the winter months. How could the dinosaurs have survived such cold weather? How did they live in the dark?

Coping With the Cold

Just how cold was it for these far-flung dinosaurs? Scientists guess that the average winter temperature in Alaska, for example, was between 36 and 43 degrees Fahrenheit when these animals were alive. (That's between 2 and 6 degrees Celsius.) And temperatures might have dipped to as low as 12 degrees Fahrenheit (-11 degrees Celsius). How can scientists guess these temperatures? They study the number of different plant fossils found in the area. The colder an area is, the fewer the kinds of plants that can grow there.

Modern animals that live in cool regions have coats of fur or feathers to keep them warm. The dinosaurs did not. Other animals make caves or holes for themselves and hibernate, or sleep, through the cold months. But the dinosaurs found in Alaska were thirty feet long! They would have needed huge holes to crawl into. The remains found in Australia's Lightning Ridge are of small animals. So far, all of them have been less than six feet long. These Australian dinosaurs might have been able to hibernate.

Some scientists think that the dinosaurs of the Far North might not have really adjusted to the cold. Instead, they might have just *migrated*, moving south during the winter months. Many animals do this today.

Reading the Temperature

Scientists don't all agree about what the temperatures in these areas were. Some say it is not possible to guess how cold it was just from plant fossils. Not all kinds of plants survive as fossils. If more types of plants grew long ago in these areas, the coldest temperature might have been 39 degrees Fahrenheit (4 degrees Celsius) instead of 12 degrees Fahrenheit (-11 degrees Celsius).

These "winter" dinosaurs are proof to some people that dinosaurs must have been warm-blooded to survive. But others say that the dinosaurs' large size protected them from sudden changes in temperature. They think that large amounts of food being digested in these huge stomachs could have made enough heat to keep the dinosaurs warm.

Be a Dinosaur Detective!

Find out for yourself what difference size can make in changing temperature. Fill both a small glass and a large glass with hot water. Take their temperatures to make sure they are the same. Leave both in a cool area for about twenty minutes. Take both their temperatures again. Which glass has lost the most heat? Why? What might this tell you about dinosaur heating systems?

Seeing in the Dark

Life at the North and South poles isn't just cold—it's dark during the winter! The sun sets earlier and rises later. For a few weeks every year, the sun does not appear at all. How did the dinosaurs cope with the long nights?

Some of the Australian dinosaurs had special features that could have helped in the dark. One kind of animal, the *hypsilophodonts* (HIP-sih-LOW-fuh-donts), had quite large eyes. Their brains were also quite large, even though their bodies were just the size of chickens. It would seem the hypsilophodonts had keen eyesight for finding their way in the moonlight.

The Traveling Dinosaur

How far did the dinosaurs roam? Did they migrate from one region to another as the seasons changed? Or did these ancient animals just wander aimlessly in search of new supplies of food? Scientists are quite sure that at least some types of dinosaurs moved fairly long distances. But they have many questions about where they came from and went to, and why. They also wonder if some dinosaur types in different parts of the world were related. Perhaps common ancestors spread to many different areas.

Dinosaur Highway

Picture a well-worn path stretching for miles. Many different kinds of animals use it from year to year. Canadian and Chinese explorers recently found sections of a dinosaur path like this in Inner Mongolia. At least four different kinds of dinosaurs had used the route. Where were they all going?

Distant Cousins

Similar kinds of dinosaurs have been found in such odd places as Alberta, Canada; Mongolia; and Antarctica. Armor-plated dinosaurs called *ankylosaurs* (ang-KILE-uh-sores), for example, have been found in Asia, Europe, Australia, and even Antarctica. Bridges of land connected the continents long ago. Dinosaurs could have walked between them.

As they spread around the world, some types of dinosaurs might have changed. They would have *adapted* to the new region they were in.

Herds and Packs

Were dinosaurs loners who kept away from each other? Did they live in small groups? Or did they travel in large herds? Track ways, such as the one found in Inner Mongolia, suggest that great numbers of the same kind of animal traveled together. Scientists think that some, like the *hadrosaurs* and horned dinosaurs, lived in small groups for part of the year. At other times, they banded into large herds and moved together. Perhaps they did this to mate or nest. Maybe it happened only when the seasons changed.

Huge fossil beds have been found with the bones of many dinosaurs of the same type, or species. This is more proof that dinosaurs lived in packs and herds. Living together has advantages. The plant-eaters could band together to protect themselves. The meat-eaters could hunt better in packs.

Animals that live together behave differently from those that live alone. They may play together. They may have ways of "talking" to one another. Some herds and packs have leaders the way wolf packs do. Was the dinosaur friendlier than we have imagined?

Family Living

Maiasaura (Mah-ee-ah-SORE-uh) returns to her nest after a morning of feeding. Inside the hollow, among the pieces of broken eggshell, are fifteen baby Maiasaura. Only a few days old, they cannot feed themselves yet. The mother's head nuzzles down among them. She opens her mouth to spit up a breakfast of well-chewed leaves and berries. The babies quickly lap it up and turn to her for another mouthful. All around, the same breakfast is taking place in a dozen other Maiasaura nests.

This is how a paleontologist named Jack Horner thinks at least one group of dinosaurs looked after their young. In 1978, he found a great nesting area of a duck-billed dinosaur he called Maiasaura. This name means "good mother lizard." The first nest Horner found held fossils of baby dinosaurs that seem to have grown while still living in the nest. Their teeth showed that they had been fed a mixture of grass, seeds, and berries.

These nests changed people's thinking about dinosaur families. Before, it was thought that dinosaurs just laid eggs, covered them over, and went away. Now, we know that some dinosaurs stayed with their young to protect and feed them.

Horner also found many other nests near the first. All together, hundreds of baby and egg fossils were found in the area. Could it be that great numbers of dinosaurs came together to nest each year?

Happy Birthday, Apatosaurus!

Another paleontologist, named Robert Bakker, has an even more amazing idea about the dinosaurs and their young. Bakker has carefully studied the way the enormous plant-eater Apatosaurus was built. He says that this creature might have been designed to give birth to living babies. He believes the newborn babies would have weighed between 200 and 300 pounds.

Some other scientists think that Bakker's idea is possible, because no one has ever found an Apatosaurus egg. They agree that being born alive would have helped Apatosaurus grow so large. A full-grown Apatosaurus was ninety feet long. You have to get an early start to grow this big! And eggs can only be so big. The largest ones found are only eight inches long. To be any bigger, they would need shells so thick a baby could not get out!

Not everyone is happy with Bakker's theory, however. Some scientists say the only sure proof would be finding the fossil of an unborn baby Apatosaurus. Bakker's answer is that an unborn baby Apatosaurus might already have been found—without people knowing it. At the start of the twentieth century, the bones of a small dinosaur were found mixed together with the bones of an adult Apatosaurus. Scientists then thought the smaller bones belonged to a different species of dinosaur. But Bakker says they may have belonged to an unborn baby growing inside the adult.

Did Apatosaurus give birth to live babies? Could other dinosaurs have done so too?

By Land or by Lake?

Imagine that millions of years from now, scientists dig up the bones of a four-legged creature with a very long neck. You and I might know it as a giraffe. But let's imagine that these scientists had never seen or heard of an animal like it. They would have no idea what kind of surroundings it lived in. Nor would they know what it used some parts of its body for.

Looking at its long neck, they might guess that it spent a lot of time in the water. Its long neck would allow it to hold its head above water to breathe. This would be a clever guess, but we know it would be wrong. Giraffes live on dry land and eat leaves off trees. Scientists of the nineteenth and twentieth centuries might have made the same kind of mistake with Apatosaurus and other giant, long-necked plant-eaters, or *sauropods*.

Tootling a Happy Tune

What about those "noses" in the air? How would they have been used by a dry-land creature? Bakker says they might have been used for "tootling," or making noise. Could those nostrils have been used like musical instruments for dinosaur songs?

Solid Footing

Many sauropods like Apatosaurus had a long neck and nostrils high up on their heads. Some of these dinosaurs had their "noses" above their eyes! Their heads seem like great submarine periscopes. So many people thought that they were well suited to paddling around in lakes or swamps. For many years, this is how these giants have been shown.

But a closer look at the feet of the Apatosaurus showed that they weren't made to carry an animal through wet muck. Animals living in wet areas often have feet that spread outward to give them support. But the Apatosaurus's feet were firm and solid like an elephant's.

Robert Bakker, the same scientist who says Apatosaurus gave birth to live babies, looked closely at where they lived. He found large lumps of limestone in the areas where the Apatosaurus fossils were found. These lumps of limestone are only found in areas that were very dry. This could mean that Apatosaurus lived in an area of *drought*, instead of lakes. Bakker paints a picture of a land-dwelling Apatosaurus. Like a giraffe, Apatosaurus used its long neck to graze the tops of trees.

The Duckbills Aren't Ducks!

Sometimes, it can be difficult to change fixed ideas. The first duck-billed dinosaur, Hadrosaurus, was found in the nineteenth century. People thought these dinosaurs lived near water. This is because the *duckbills* had jaws shaped like ducks' beaks.

Some scientists suspected the duckbills might have lived on dry land. Their jaws contained many rows of teeth. These would have been useful for grinding at the kinds of tough trees and bushes found in a forest. The mushy plants of swamps and lakes could be eaten without all those teeth!

It was much later that scientists were sure the duckbills could live on dry land. The proof lay in the stomach of a duckbill *mummy*. Usually, fossils are made up only of bones. But when a dead animal becomes dried out, or mummified, it still carries the soft parts of its body, such as skin and tendons. When the mummy of the duckbill Anatosaurus (Ah-NAT-uh-SORE-us) was found, it still carried its last dinner in its stomach. Instead of soft water plants, Anatosaurus had eaten forest foods like pine needles and cones.

The duckbills might have been good swimmers just the same. Their long, flat tails would have helped them in the water, where they could escape hungry meat-eaters.

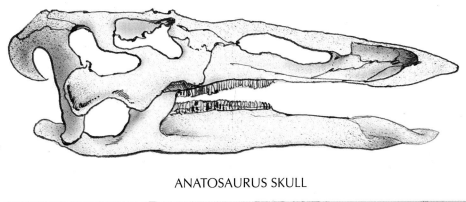

ANATOSAURUS SKULL

Today's Dinosaurs— On the Wing

Look up in the sky or at the high branches of a tree. Could the little feathered creatures there be modern dinosaurs? Scientists once thought that the dinosaur family came to a dead end sixty-five million years ago. But now it seems that at least some dinosaurs have lived on—as birds!

Ancient Wing

In 1861, the bones of a small, light creature were discovered in a German mine. In many ways, it was like the small, meat-eating dinosaurs such as Coelophysis (See-low-FISE-iss) or Velociraptor (Veh-loss-ih-RAP-tor). But the rock around the fossils was covered with the marks of ancient wing, tail, and body feathers. And so this new creature was given the name Archaeopteryx (Ar-kee-OP-ter-ix). It means "ancient wing."

Archaeopteryx was the first possible link between dinosaurs and birds. Like the dinosaurs, it had a toothy jaw, long tail, and claws on its feet. It also had claws on its wings. Like the birds, Archaeopteryx had light bones and feathers. But its wings probably did not make it a good flyer. Archaeopteryx's breast muscles were not strong enough to flap the wings very hard.

Scientists formed the theory that Archaeopteryx was the ancestor of modern birds. Since then, many people have thought of "ancient wing" as the missing link between birds and dinosaurs.

Sorry—Too Young

Not everyone was sure of the link between Archaeopteryx and today's birds. Modern birds such as gulls and herons appeared only a few million years after Archaeopteryx. This was too little time for so many changes to happen. Animal species take much longer to change. Archaeopteryx, at only 150 million years old, was just too young to be the ancestor of modern birds!

Another Ancient Flyer

New fossils have been found recently that might have been the missing link. Protoavis (Pro-toe-AV-iss) is another dinosaur that might have had wings. But so far, no one has found a complete skeleton. The bones that have been found are small and light like a bird's. Some scientists are convinced that Protoavis is a true bird ancestor. Protoavis is seventy-five million years older than Archaeopteryx. It would have had time to change into modern birds.

Like Archaeopteryx, Protoavis had a long tail and legs built for running. But its breastbone was more like a bird's. It was better built for holding strong wing muscles. Protoavis's eyes and ears were also more like a bird's than a dinosaur's.

But the Protoavis fossil is missing one important part—feathers. This makes some scientists doubt that it was a link to the birds. Is it possible that Protoavis did have feathers but left no trace of them? Or was Protoavis just another small, meat-eating dinosaur?

23

The Tale of the Troödon

We don't often think of dinosaurs as smart. Many people still think they were an odd group of slow-witted reptiles. And dinosaurs are rarely thought of as being like humans in any way. But at least one scientist thinks that a certain kind of dinosaur was quite smart and shared some features with humans.

The 'Handy' Dinosaur

In 1968, a scientist named Dale Russell found some bones of a small, meat-eating dinosaur called Stenonychosaurus (Sten-ON-ik-uh-SORE-us). Its name means "narrow-clawed lizard." This dinosaur's skull showed that it had been small, but with a large brain. The skull also showed that Stenonychosaurus's eyesight worked like ours. Stenonychosaurus also had hands that resembled humans'.

It had thumbs that could be turned inwards to grasp things. This is unusual among animals.

Russell put together a startling model of Stenonychosaurus. He showed it standing upright, like a human. The model was four feet tall and weighed about ninety pounds. Russell called this human-like model a dinosaurid (die-no-SORE-id). People were amazed by this dinosaur, which seemed so advanced for its time.

Whoops! Wrong Dinosaur

Paleontologist Jack Horner later showed that Russell's model was wrong. Horner also found a fossil skull of Stenonychosaurus. But this one was more complete. It had teeth—the same teeth as another small meat-eater called Troödon (TRUE-oh-don). This new skull showed that Stenonychosaurus and Troödon were the same creature! People had known of Troödon for many years. It was considered one of the bird-like ostrich dinosaurs.

Another Troödon skull was found in Canada by a scientist named Phillip Currie. It shows even more clearly how this dinosaur was like modern birds. The bones of its inner ear were very much like a bird's.

What should we make of the Troödon? Is it sure proof of a link between dinosaurs and birds? Or does Troödon show that, given time, dinosaurs might one day have become as intelligent as humans?

Dinosaur Brains

Just how smart were the dinosaurs? Some of the giant dinosaurs survived with brains no bigger than walnuts! Seventy-foot-long Apatosaurus had a brain about the same size as a cat's.

In comparison, Troödon had a brain about as large as an ostrich's. The ostrich is the world's largest living bird. It and the Troödon are about the same size.

Using Their Heads

What does it mean to be a "smart" dinosaur? Scientists think the clever ones had well-developed eyesight and hearing. Some might have had a keen sense of smell. These smarter animals also would have had better control over their limbs. Troödon, for example, was probably very good with its hands!

The smart dinosaurs would have been better equipped for hunting. Many of the meat-eaters had large heads. Tyrannosaurus (Tie-RAN-uh-SORE-us), probably one of the greatest hunters, had a huge head and quite a large brain. Many of the gentle plant-eaters had tiny heads on top of enormous bodies. Giant sauropods such as Apatosaurus and Diplodocus (Dih-PLOD-uh-kus) were probably quite slow-witted.

Some of the cleverest dinosaurs might have been the egg-stealers such as Oviraptor (Oh-vee-RAP-tor). These creatures had to react quickly to escape angry mothers trying to protect their eggs. Sneaking up on a nest is no easy trick when it is guarded by a Triceratops (Try-SAIR-uh-tops) the size of a bus!

One Brain or Two?

Did some kinds of dinosaurs have two brains to make up for their brains' small size? This was once thought to be true for Stegosaurus. This thirty-foot-long dinosaur had a bundle of nerves at the bottom of its spine. This "mini-brain" probably helped it to control its hind legs and tail. Since the brain up front was so small, maybe Stegosaurus needed help in the rear! Stegosaurus used its spiked tail to protect itself. The hind end of the beast would have to "think" fast!

But the nerve center near the tail was not a real brain. It was just a helper to control muscle movement. Other large dinosaurs might have had nerve bundles like this near their tails as well.

Too Dumb to Survive?

Why the dinosaurs disappeared so suddenly is one of the world's greatest mysteries. Some people think the dinosaurs simply became too dumb! As the creatures grew larger and larger, perhaps their brains did not keep up with their bodies.

But huge dinosaurs like Brachiosaurus and Diplodocus succeeded for tens of millions of years. Remains of Stegosaurus have been found that show this species survived almost fifty million years! Modern human beings and our earliest ancestors have only been around for about three million years. Will we be smart enough to survive as long as the dinosaurs?

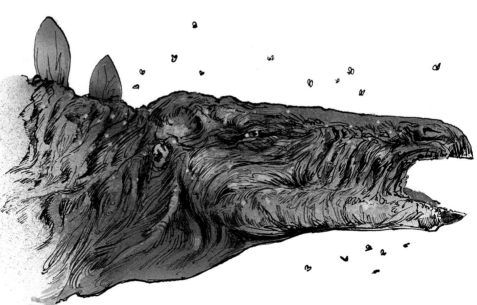

Dinosaur Colors

Picture a bright green Tyrannosaurus with red spots down its back. How about a black-and-white duckbill striped like a zebra? We usually picture these creatures in drab grays or browns. That's because we have thought of dinosaurs as overgrown lizards for so long. But scientists don't really know what color dinosaurs were. This is because so little has survived of dinosaur skin. The bone fossils can tell us how dinosaurs were built, but not really how they were "dressed."

Dressing to Fit In

Like most animals, dinosaurs were probably colored to blend in with their surroundings. This would have helped them to hide from their enemies. Gentle plant-eaters especially must keep out of sight. They have little hope of fighting to protect themselves.

Dinosaurs who lived in dry areas may have been colored like many desert animals of today. An Ankylosaurus (Ang-KILE-uh-SORE-us) who was light brown would have faded into a sandy background. A tree-grazing Apatosaurus might have been colored in shades of green and brown. But no one can be sure. Scientists cannot agree yet on the type of surroundings some dinosaurs lived in.

Eye-Catching Outfits

Not all animals use their coloring just for protection. Some seem to want to stand out in the crowd. Peacocks with their bright feathers, tropical fish with their brilliant scales—these creatures are not trying to hide! Why do they risk their lives to get attention? The answer is to attract other members of their own kind.

Just like some humans who dye their hair or wear bright clothes, some dinosaurs might have been eye-catchers. Could Triceratops's great bony frill have been bright red or blue? Maybe Deinonychus was spotted like a leopard. The way these dinosaurs looked could have been used to catch a mate's attention. Or maybe it just helped these dinosaurs spot their own kind.

The only real evidence scientists have about dinosaur colors is the dried skin of a duckbill mummy. The entire body of an Anatosaurus has survived hundreds of millions of years. Its skin is covered with small, faded freckles. Could these once have been a dazzling display of brilliant colors?

When Did the Dinosaurs Disappear?

Whatever killed off the dinosaurs seems to have happened suddenly, about sixty-five million years ago. That is when the last fossils date from. At least, that is what scientists agreed on—until recently. A group of scientists have a new theory about the end of the dinosaurs. They say these animals did not all die at the same time. Instead, the Age of Dinosaurs ended slowly over millions of years.

Fewer and Fewer Dinosaurs

We usually think of the dinosaurs being wiped out while they were at the peak of their development. But scientists studying bones in Montana think dinosaurs were dying off before sixty-five million years ago. These scientists say that in the last million years of the dinosaur age, the number of dinosaur types probably dropped greatly. They think the dinosaurs were dying off because of a change in the weather. Plant fossils from the time show the climate was getting cooler.

Other scientists disagree with this theory. They say that the bones studied in Montana were too badly broken to be solid evidence. They say we can't be sure about the variety of dinosaurs these bones and teeth were from.

Dinosaur Survivors

Still other scientists say they have found dinosaur fossils that are less than sixty-five million years old. Were these from survivors who lived on after the other dinosaurs became extinct? These "young" bones have been found in China and Montana. Some are from almost a million years after the dinosaurs were supposed to have disappeared.

Not everyone is convinced. Remember that the age of fossils is mostly determined from the layer of the earth that they are found in. Some say that the "young" fossils are, in fact, old fossils. They might somehow have been moved to a different layer of the earth. The earth around them might have worn away long ago, leaving them above ground. Water might have moved them to a newer part of the earth's surface. Anyone who later discovered the fossils would think the fossils had died at that time in the earth's history.

So did the dinosaurs die all together in one mysterious disaster? Or did they die over many years, as the earth's climate cooled? Whatever caused their death did not kill off all other animals. Among the survivors were the early mammals. With their biggest competitors wiped out, these small, warm-blooded creatures have thrived ever since.

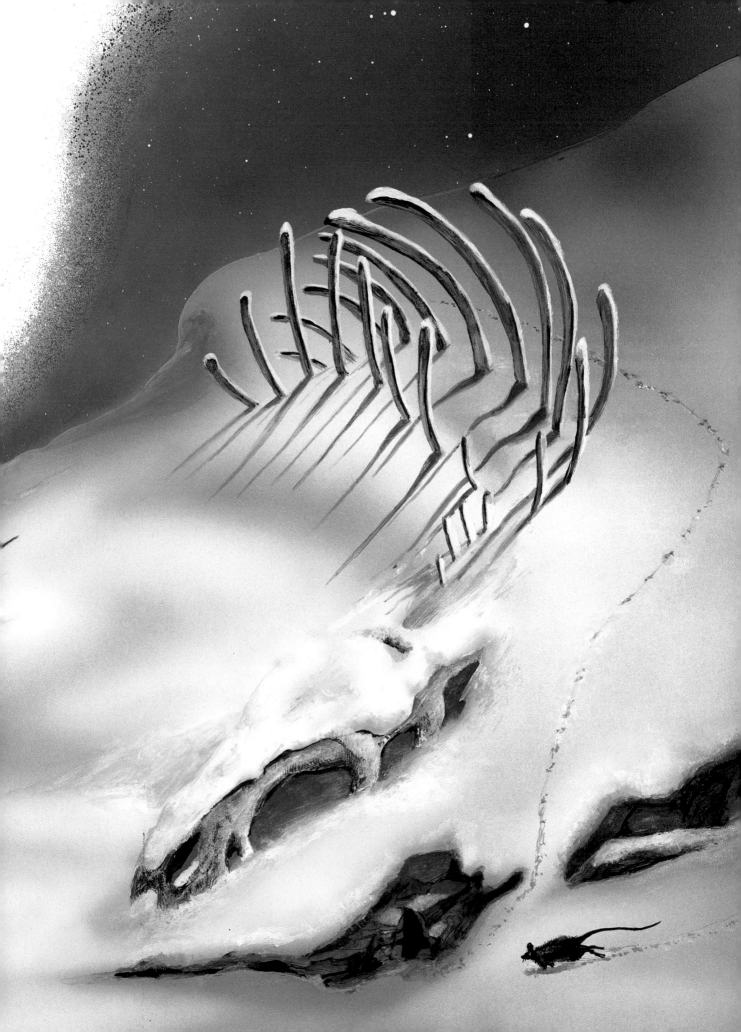

Glossary

adaptation The process of changing to fit an environment, or conditons that surround us.

amphibians Cold-blooded animals that live part of their life on land and part in water.

ankylosaurs Group of bird-hipped dinosaurs that featured a body covering of thick armor.

climates The year-round weather conditions of different regions.

continents The earth's main bodies of land: Europe, Asia, Africa, North America, South America, Antarctica, and Australia.

drought Long, dry period.

duckbills Common name for the hadrosaurs, a group of dinosaurs with jaws shaped like ducks' bills.

ectotherms Cold-blooded animals; must get their heat from the surroundings.

endotherms Warm-blooded animals; able to produce their own body heat.

fossil Plant or animal remain hardened in rock.

hadrosaurs Group of dinosaurs known as the duckbills because their jaws resembled ducks' bills.

hypsilophodonts Group of bird-hipped dinosaurs with large eyes and brains but small bodies.

mammals Warm-blooded animals; feed their young with milk.

Mesozoic Earth's "middle years"; era in history between 225 and 65 million years ago.

migration The process of moving from one region to another.

mummy Body preserved for a long time either by drying or by other special means.

paleontologists Scientists who study fossils of forms of life that existed long ago.

reptiles Cold-blooded, egg-laying animals with backbones.

sauropods Large, plant-eating, lizard-hipped group of dinosaurs.